SHOCKZONE™
GAMES AND GAMERS

THE BRAIN-BOOSTING BENEFITS OF GAMING

ARIE KAPLAN

Lerner Publications Company • Minneapolis

NOTE TO READERS: Not all games are appropriate for players of all ages. Remember to follow video game rating systems and the advice of a parent or guardian when deciding which games to play.

Lerner Publications Company
A division of Lerner Publishing Group, Inc.
241 First Avenue North
Minneapolis, MN 55401 U.S.A.

Website address: www.lernerbooks.com

Content Consultant: Crystle Martin, postdoctoral researcher, Digital Media and Learning Hub at the University of California, Irvine

Library of Congress Cataloging-in-Publication Data

Kaplan, Arie.
    The brain-boosting benefits of gaming / by Arie Kaplan.
        pages   cm. — (Shockzone—games and gamers)
    Includes index.
    ISBN 978-1-4677-1251-4 (lib. bdg. : alk. paper)
    ISBN 978-1-4677-1781-6 (eBook)
    1. Video games—Juvenile literature. I. Title.
    GV1469.3K347 2014
    794.8—dc23   2013005139

Manufactured in the United States of America
1 – MG – 7/15/13

TABLE OF CONTENTS

LEARNING TO PLAY AND PLAYING TO LEARN

When you think of video games, you think of entertainment. And there's a good reason for that. Gaming probably makes you think of flashy action, tricky puzzles, and high scores. **But if you think that all games can do is entertain, think again.** Games are being used today to teach and train all kinds of people, from students to doctors to soldiers.

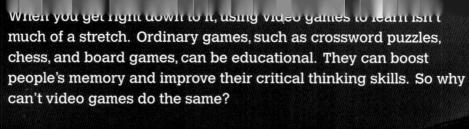

When you get right down to it, using video games to learn isn't much of a stretch. Ordinary games, such as crossword puzzles, chess, and board games, can be educational. They can boost people's memory and improve their critical thinking skills. So why can't video games do the same?

As it turns out, games are an awesome tool for teaching and training people. The best educational games combine entertainment and learning. They make information more interesting, so students actually want to learn more. And because tons of people already love gaming, it's a natural way to teach all kinds of things to them. Having fun and learning at the same time? Definitely a win-win situation.

It may surprise you, but games can be a great way to make learning more fun.

HOW VIDEO GAMES TEACH

For a long time, many teachers thought of video games as "the enemy." They thought games distracted students from learning, pulling them away from their real work. But now, many educators are seeing video games as an exciting new teaching tool. Why the change? As it turns out, games and schools have more in common than you might think.

Think for a minute about how school works. You try to get the best scores you can on assignments. Once in a while you use what you've learned to ace tests. Eventually you move on to the next grade. Well, this is pretty much the same stuff you do in video games. Think of school tests as basically major bad guys you have to battle. Getting a good score on your test is like a high score in a game. And the different grades in school are like stages in a game.

Teachers have figured out this connection, and they're using it to get kids more excited about learning. The name for this connection is gamification. (Yep, that's actually what it's called).

gamification = making everyday activities more like video games

How would this work? There are tons of ways to do it. Teachers can track student test scores just like experience points in a role-playing game. In this kind of game, getting these points allows you to "level up," boosting your character's power. But in school, "leveling up" could mean winning a reward, such as extra credit or extra game time. Just like in a game, players could compete against classmates to try to get their name on a high score chart. If you want to get these rewards, you might find yourself studying more for a big test.

No longer will gaming in class get you in trouble. Games might now be a part of your assignment.

Gamification helps people who love playing video games stay motivated. It all comes down to a chemical in our brains called dopamine. Whenever we achieve something—even if it's just something little—dopamine is released in the brain. As the chemical flows through that squishy gray matter in your head, it gives you a sense of pleasure and happiness.

Back when we were cave people, dopamine helped us feel good about escaping from a fierce saber-toothed tiger or a lumbering wooly mammoth. Our brains wanted to keep feeling good, so we avoided becoming prehistoric snack food. Even though we don't have to dodge bloody fangs on

When you beat a level in a game, dopamine flows through your brain and makes you feel good.

a daily basis anymore, the dopamine system still makes us feel good. In modern times, it happens when we do simpler stuff. Landing a skateboard trick or a gymnastics move, beating the final level in *New Super Mario Bros. U*, and getting an A on a test—all of these things release dopamine into the brain.

When teachers add more goals into their classes, dopamine is released in students' brains more often. After this, their brains naturally look for chances to keep making it happen more frequently. This keeps students interested as they try to complete more and more achievements. Whether you're playing a game or taking a test, remember that dopamine is what helps you stay motivated. And be thankful you're sitting in school rather than running away from a saber-toothed tiger.

Getting any kind of high score releases dopamine in the brain, encouraging you to keep doing well.

A SUPER-QUICK HISTORY OF EDUCATIONAL GAMES

Many teachers have only started using video games and gamification in their classrooms pretty recently. But educational video games are nothing new. In fact, they've been around since the early days of video games themselves. Let's take a look at some of the top educational games ever made. These games were fun and exciting—and sometimes, just plain weird. But they all made learning more interesting than ever before.

One of the earliest educational games was *Lemonade Stand*. It came out in the late 1970s for the Apple II computer, the great-great

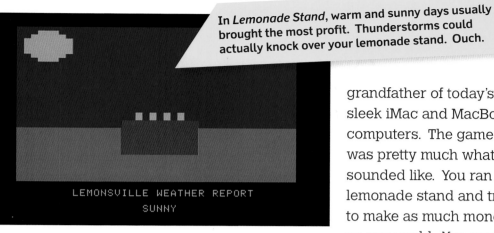

LEMONSVILLE WEATHER REPORT
SUNNY

grandfather of today's sleek iMac and MacBook computers. The game was pretty much what it sounded like. You ran a lemonade stand and tried to make as much money as you could. You could make decisions to save money, like putting less sugar in each cup. But if customers complained, you could end up selling fewer cups overall. It was fairly simple, but it taught players about the basic ideas of economics.

Another important educational game came out in 1986: *Number Munchers*. It was definitely a bit weirder than *Lemonade Stand*. In *Number Munchers*, you play as a strange green creature that basically looks like a mouth with legs. You move across a grid of numbers, eating any that match that level's rule. For example, on a level that tells you to munch even numbers, you'd chomp down on 2 and 4, but not 7. The whole time, you also have to avoid monsters that try to munch on you. Despite the weirdness—or maybe because of the weirdness—kids loved the game.

economics = the study of businesses and money

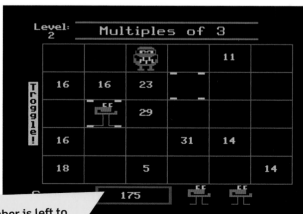

Paris
Monday, 1 p.m.

France, with a population of about 55 million, is famous for its food, wine, fashion and art.

Where in the World Is Carmen Sandiego? taught students about geography while they helped solve the case of an international crime spree.

 SEE

 DEPART

 CRIME

Another hit educational game from the 1980s was the classic *Where in the World Is Carmen Sandiego?* What *Lemonade Stand* and *Number Munchers* did for business and math, *Carmen Sandiego* did for geography. Players tracked the thief Carmen Sandiego and her minions across the globe, figuring out clues to discover where she was traveling next. The puns and humor in the game kept players interested. And the whole time, they were learning all about foreign countries and regions.

But educational games weren't just for regular school subjects. They also helped teach kids how to use the computers themselves. Ordinarily, learning to type on a keyboard can be pretty boring. But games to teach typing skills can make it surprisingly fun. Some of them combined typing with other things kids were interested in, such as sports and other video games. *Slam Dunk Typing* made players type words correctly in order to pass or shoot a basketball. *Mario Teaches Typing* let gamers play as Nintendo's popular Mario character, typing letters to break blocks and knock over bad guys.

dad EADE lad j

Mario Teaches Typing took players to familiar locations from *Mario* games but added typing practice to the mix.

But one typing game towered over the others in its sheer weirdness: *Typing of the Dead*. Most zombie games have you use guns or other weapons to defeat crowds of zombies. But not this one. Instead, you type words and letters as fast as you can to blow the zombies to bits. Totally weird? Yep. But totally educational and fun too. Just like all good educational games, *Typing of the Dead* combines the exciting action of games with learning and training. It works for schools, the military, companies, and even for doctors. So the next time you play an educational game, keep in mind that you're experiencing the future of learning.

GAMING FOR GRADES:
Games in Schools

Imagine going to school and doing nothing but playing video games all day during class ... and not getting in trouble! Crazy, right?

You might think so. But if you're in Al Doyle's class, you just might get an A for playing video games. Doyle teaches his students about video games and technology. Students play games, then think about them. For example, they might watch how an enemy in a game moves. Then they use graph paper to draw the movement and figure out the enemy's pattern. You're probably already wondering, "Where is this amazing school?" Good question.

Doyle teaches at a school in New York City called Quest to Learn. The school was designed to use games in the classroom. In fact, it was even founded by video game designer Katie Salen.

Salen realized that kids love to play video games outside of school. But she also realized many kids weren't as excited about learning during school. So she connected the dots. Her goal is to make kids feel more passionate about learning. She connects education to the things they already like to do. The key to this plan? Video games.

Some schools in Japan have started using the handheld Nintendo DS console in the classroom.

CLASSES AT QUEST TO LEARN

The classes at Quest to Learn may cover normal topics, but they do it in a totally radical way. Instead of math class, students have a class called Codeworlds. While designing games and completing quests, students learn all about numbers and what they mean. And in a class called Sports for the Mind, students can create their own levels in popular games like *Minecraft* and *Portal 2*.

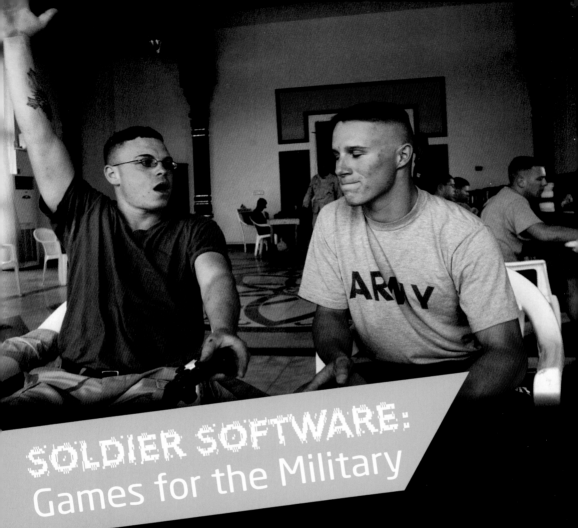

SOLDIER SOFTWARE:
Games for the Military

Video games became hugely popular more than thirty years ago. That means a large number of today's adults grew up with video games. And that includes members of today's military. With many men and women in the military being gamers, what better way to train them than with video games?

One of the toughest parts about being in the military can be living and working in foreign countries. If you don't know the language and the local customs, everyday life may be difficult. The U.S. Army created the video game *Tactical Iraqi* to help solve this problem for

MILITARY CONTROLLERS

When the military developed robots that could fly through the air or could drive across the ground, it also had to think of how soldiers would control the robots. The military quickly realized that many people are already familiar with video game controllers. As a result, many controllers for these robots look and feel almost the same as the controllers for popular video game consoles such as the Xbox 360 and Wii.

soldiers traveling to Iraq. The game includes language training in Arabic as well as a guide to local greetings and signs of respect.

It also helps soldiers train for tense situations. In one level, you play as Sergeant Smith, an American soldier in Iraq. You're looking for information, so you and your soldiers decide to enter a café to ask people questions. Do you barge in yelling with your gun out? If so, people aren't likely to help you. But if you remove your helmet and treat the café customers respectfully, they'll probably cooperate.

By combining basic language skills with problem solving under pressure, soldiers learn to avoid embarrassing or even dangerous situations. And it's all because of a video game.

The *Tactical Iraqi* training game has been used since 2005.

UNDER THE (VIRTUAL) KNIFE: Games and Surgeons

Think about the skills you need to be a surgeon. **A steady hand. Quick reflexes. Agile fingers.**

Now think about the skills you need to be a master video game player. Hmm ... Can you see where this is going?

You guessed it. Video games, it turns out, can be a great way for surgeons to get better at their jobs. Back in 2002, a surgeon who was also a gamer thought there might be something to this idea. To test it, he set up an experiment.

First, he had surgeons play the game *Super Monkey Ball.* In this wacky puzzle game, players control monkeys rolling around in clear plastic balls. They must navigate the monkeys through tricky mazes and across narrow platforms. Beating the game's levels requires very precise controller movements.

Next, the surgeons took tests to check their surgery skills. The results? The surgeons who did better at the game made fewer mistakes and worked much faster. Not only that, but surgeons who played video games regularly also scored better on the test. The next time you're at the hospital, you might want to ask your surgeon if she's a gamer.

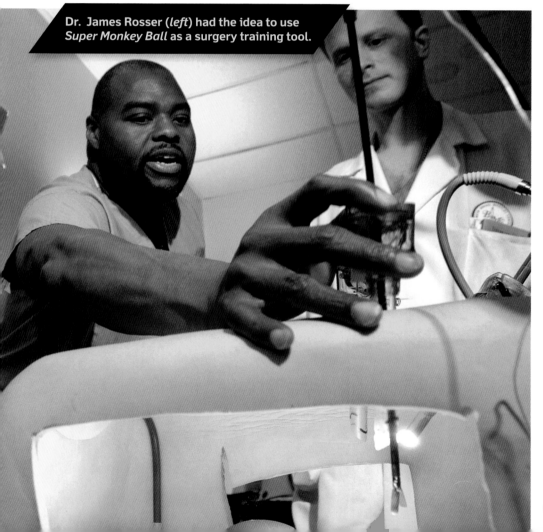

Dr. James Rosser (*left*) had the idea to use *Super Monkey Ball* as a surgery training tool.

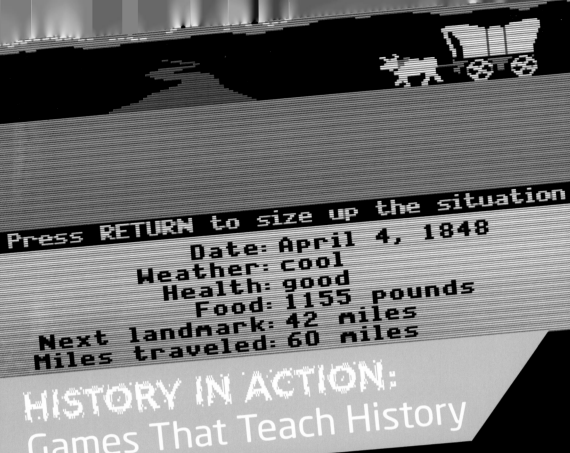

Press RETURN to size up the situation
Date: April 4, 1848
Weather: cool
Health: good
Food: 1155 pounds
Next landmark: 42 miles
Miles traveled: 60 miles

HISTORY IN ACTION:
Games That Teach History

Ever heard of the Oregon Trail? It was a path from Missouri to Oregon that settlers took way back in the 1800s. If you weren't killed by disease on the trail, you might freeze to death. If you managed to stay warm, you could still drown in a river, be crushed by a wagon, or get bitten by a snake. To sum it all up, the trail was **unbelievably harsh.**

Oh yeah—it also made for a great video game.

The Oregon Trail came out in 1971. All the brutality of the real-life trail was carried over to the game. It was a huge hit with gamers. People loved stocking up their wagons with stacks of supplies, then setting out for Oregon. They enjoyed hunting for buffalo, bears, and rabbits to increase their food supply. They had fun stopping at

Age of Empires III, the latest game in the series, lets players advance all the way to the 1800s and add cannons and riflemen to their armies.

trading posts to fix their wagons. And they even liked writing the words for the tombstone when a member of their group died of dysentery. Even though they were having fun, players were learning about how rough life had been on the real Oregon Trail.

Other games helped history come to life too. The *Age of Empires* series, which started in 1997, taught gamers about ancient warfare. Beginning in the Stone Age, players advanced through history. In the first part of the game, your army might be a small group of dudes carrying clubs. But by the end, you could have a huge army with swords, crossbows, and catapults. Once again, gamers were playing and learning at the same time.

SKY SCHOOL: Learning to Fly with Video Games

There's a good reason why new pilots don't start learning to fly in real airplanes. One mistake and your shiny new plane is a pile of smoking wreckage. But if you can't learn to fly in a plane, how can you learn to fly at all? The answer: video games.

New pilots use video games called flight simulators to learn the basics of flying a plane. That way, messing up doesn't have deadly consequences. The flight simulators used by big companies and the military are amazingly realistic. And equally expensive. You sit in a replica cockpit, surrounded by realistic controls. All the airplane's windows are actually big screens, showing what would be outside if you were really flying. The fanciest simulators sit on special platforms that can move around when you use the controls.

But what if you can't afford a million-dollar simulator and you're still interested in learning to fly? No problem. Flight simulator games you can play at home have been around for years. They may not be quite as advanced as the best flight simulators. Still, the incredible power of modern computers has made them pretty impressive.

The first home flight simulator games were super primitive. The scenery? A black background with white lines. The dashboard? Purple, green, and black lines and shapes. And when you crashed, a comic book word bubble popped up that said "CRASH." Fast forward to today. With a good computer, home flight simulators can look stunning. Shimmering water, fluffy clouds, and shiny airplanes can make you feel as though you're really flying. And if you crash, you can just restart the game.

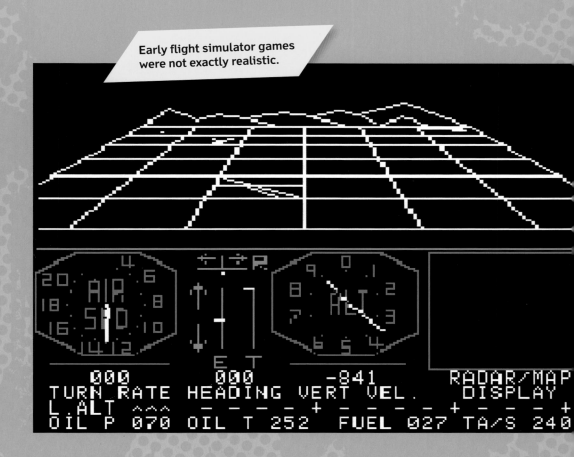

Early flight simulator games were not exactly realistic.

IN GOOD COMPANY:
How Corporations Use Games

Imagine you're running a company. Your employees all love to play video games. In fact, they grew up playing them. So when it comes time to train them for their jobs, how will you do it? A long lecture? Maybe a sleepy slide show? Or a monotonous movie? No, no, and no. What you need is a video game.

Many companies are already doing exactly that. One ice-cream store created a game for its employees to teach them how much ice cream to serve in each cone. Players have to race against the clock to scoop as many of the tasty treats as they can. At the same time, they have to make sure not to make any cones overflow with ice

For workers who grew up as gamers, playing video games for training can be a huge improvement over boring meetings.

cream. As it turned out, the company's employees loved the game. Almost one-third of all their employees downloaded it and played it voluntarily.

Games are used for tougher jobs too. One company decided to make a game to help its workers practice building computer networks. Normally the task of connecting computers together can be slow, quiet, and even boring. But not in the world of video games. The game transported the workers to the middle of a huge sandstorm on Mars. Suddenly, the ordinary job became a science-fiction adventure. And because they were absorbed in the game, players learned new information without even realizing it.

computer networks = many computers connected together to share information

ARE WII FIT OR NOT?: Exercising Your Brain and Body

Want to keep your brain healthy? Then don't forget to exercise your body too. Scientists have found out that exercise increases blood flow to the brain, helps you think more clearly, and makes you feel more focused. Ordinary exercise can give you these benefits. But what if you combined exercise with gamification? Enter *Wii Fit*.

Nintendo released the game *Wii Fit* for its Wii console in 2008. It comes with a special device called a Balance Board that looks a bit like a bathroom scale. When you stand on it while playing, it measures your weight and your balance. *Wii Fit* includes a bunch of games that use the Balance Board's abilities. In a game where you have to play as a soccer goalie, players shift their weight from

Nintendo mastermind Shigeru Miyamoto shows off *Wii Fit* in 2008.

side to side to block the ball. In a dancing game, players step on and off the board in time with the rhythm.

When gamers work out many days in a row or try new exercises for the first time, they receive in-game rewards. This can help motivate players to keep exercising. Not only do they continue to get rewards, but they also get in shape in the process.

EXPERTS AND EXERCISE GAMES

Even experts think exercise games can help kids get in better shape. In a newspaper interview, athlete Cathy Adolph said, "for a beginner or inactive kids, it's a great way to start." By the way, Adolph completed a race that included a 2.4-mile (3.9-kilometer) swim, a 112-mile (180 km) bike ride, and then a 26.2-mile (42 km) run. And she's done it twice. Clearly, she knows what she's talking about.

GAME SCHOOL:
Three Subjects You Can Learn with Games

Learn Statistics with *Pokémon*

Even if you haven't played a *Pokémon* game, you've probably at least heard of the series. Players collect and battle a huge variety of monsters. But what you may not know is that the games can teach you a lot about statistics, the study of organizing numbers and information. Here's how. Every monster in the game has a set of numbers. The numbers represent its attack power, its defense, its speed, and all kinds of other things. When you battle monsters

with someone else, it's actually the numbers that are doing the battling. You may see fireballs and energy beams shooting across the screen, but the numbers decide who's going to win. The higher your numbers, the more likely you are to be victorious. So if you want to be the very best, keep an eye on those numbers.

Learn Space Flight with *Kerbal Space Program*

Have you ever wanted to be an astronaut? If so, you might have realized that it's a hard job to get. Years of hard work and lots of luck are needed. But you can get a head start with *Kerbal Space Program*. In the game, you can build your own rockets, then fly them into space. From there, you can journey to other moons, planets, and stars. Still, it won't be easy. The game is very realistic, so actually flying to other planets will take more than pointing your ship toward where you want to go and blasting your rocket. You'll have to make tiny adjustments to speed and direction. One

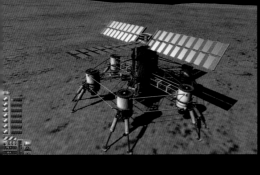

wrong move could send you shooting into deep space. And it would probably help to read a book about actual space travel. But if you can manage it, *Kerbal Space Program* is basically an introductory class to spaceflight.

Learn History with *Assassin's Creed III*

No game set in the past is completely historically accurate. But *Assassin's Creed III* might be the closest yet. The game is set in colonial America, during the 1700s. The game creators could have given the characters funny hats and old-fashioned muskets and called it a day. But instead, they spent tons of time researching the time period. They looked through historical records to see what buildings actually looked like back then. They found out how people talked. And they even hired a historian to make sure things in the game were accurate.

As a result, the game really makes you feel as though you've stepped back in time. So even while gamers have exciting adventures as an assassin, they're learning history. (*Assassin's Creed III* is rated M for Mature.)

Corbett, Sara. "Learning by Playing: Video Games in the Classroom."
http://www.nytimes.com/2010/09/19/magazine/19video-t
.html?pagewanted=all
At the beginning of the 2010 school year, a reporter went to check out Quest
to Learn. Read her article to learn lots more about the school. You can also
check out a bunch of pictures of kids playing video games in their classes.

Heick, Terry. *A Brief History of Video Games in Education*
http://www.teachthought.com/video-games-2/a-brief-history-of-video
-games-in-education
Check out this awesome list of some of the top educational games ever.
Each game entry also has a link to extra information on the game, making
this a one-stop shop for educational game info and pictures.

Kaplan, Arie. *The Crazy Careers of Video Game Designers.* Minneapolis:
Lerner Publications, 2014.
Playing video games all day sounds like an easy job. But what do combat
designers, game writers, and programmers really do? Read this book to find
out about these and other jobs in the video game industry.

Martin, Crystle. *Information Literacy, Connected Learning, and World of
Warcraft*
http://clrn.dmlhub.net/content/information-literacy-connected-learning
-and-world-warcraft
Games like *World of Warcraft* are filled with tons of characters, places, and
items. How do gamers find the info they need? Check out this article to
learn how gamers develop a skill known as information literacy, or being
able to sort through huge amounts of info quickly.

Ore, Jonathan. *Interview: Assassin's Creed III Historian Maxime
Durand*
http://dorkshelf.com/2012/11/27/interview-assassins-creed-3-historian
-maxime-durand
Check out this interview with the historian who worked on *Assassin's
Creed III* to learn how the game makers were able to make the game so
historically accurate. Warning: you might end up learning something
from the interview itself!

LERNER

SOURCE

Expand learning beyond the printed book. Download free, complementary educational resources for this book from our website, www.lerneresource.com.

The images in this book are used with the permission of: © iStockphoto/Thinkstock, p. 4; © 1MoreCreative/iStockphoto, p. 5; © Lisa F. Young/Shutterstock Images, p. 6; © Blend Images/Thinkstock, p. 7; © iStockphoto/Thinkstock, p. 8; © BKMC Photography/Shutterstock Images, p. 9; © AP Images, p. 10; Red Line Editorial, pp. 11 (top), 11 (bottom), 12, 13, 20, 21, 23, 28, 29 (top); © Rob Densmore, Laramie Daily Boomerang/AP Images, p. 14; © Katsumi Kasahara/AP Images, p. 15; © Karel Prinsloo/AP Images, p. 16; © Don Emmert/AFP/Getty Images, p. 17; © Jochen Sands/ Thinkstock, p. 18; © Adam Rountree/AP Images, p. 19; © Bernd Wuestneck/picture-alliance/dpa/AP Images, p. 22; © ImageryMajestic/Shutterstock Images, p. 24; © Pressmaster/Shutterstock Images, p. 25; © Shea Walsh/AP Images for Nintendo, p. 26; © Tina Fineberg/AP Images, p. 27; © Ubisoft/AP Images, p. 29 (bottom).

Front cover: U.S. Army Photo.

Main body text set in Calvert MT Std Regular 11/16.
Typeface provided by Monotype Typography.